The Housewarming

A play

Arthur Aldrich

Samuel French—London
New York-Toronto-Hollywood

© 1994 BY SAMUEL FRENCH

Rights of Performance by Amateurs are controlled by Samuel French Ltd, 52 Fitzroy Street, London W1P 6JR, and they, or their authorized agents, issue licences to amateurs on payment of a fee. **It is an infringement of the Copyright to give any performance or public reading of the play before the fee has been paid and the licence issued.**
The Royalty Fee indicated below is subject to contract and subject to variation at the sole discretion of Samuel French Ltd.

> Basic fee for each and every
> performance by amateurs   Code D
> in the British Isles

The publication of this play does not imply that it is necessarily available for performance by amateurs or professionals, either in the British Isles or Overseas. Amateurs and professionals considering a production are strongly advised in their own interests to apply to the appropriate agents for consent before starting rehearsals or booking a theatre or hall.

ESSEX COUNTY LIBRARY

ISBN 0 573 12049 8

Please see page iv for further copyright information

JT47430

THE HOUSEWARMING

First performed by the Wheatsheaf Players (Coventry) at the Phoenix Arts Centre, Leicester, on 7th June 1992, with the following cast:

Beattie Gladwin	Nan Bellew
Polly Bradbury	Irene Sadler
Michelle Druitt	Debbie Appelbee
Brian Martin	Jeff Wilson

Directed by Fred Walton

COPYRIGHT INFORMATION
(See also page ii)

This play is fully protected under the Copyright Laws of the British Commonwealth of Nations, the United States of America and all countries of the Berne and Universal Copyright Conventions.

All rights, including Stage, Motion Picture, Radio, Television, Public Reading, and Translation into Foreign Languages, are strictly reserved.

No part of this publication may lawfully be reproduced in ANY form or by any means — photocopying, typescript, recording (including video-recording), manuscript, electronic, mechanical, or otherwise — or be transmitted or stored in a retrieval system, without prior permission.

Rights of Performance by Amateurs are controlled by Samuel French Ltd, 52 Fitzroy Street, London W1P 6JR, and they, or their authorized agents, issue licences to amateurs on payment of a fee. **It is an infringement of the Copyright to give any performance or public reading of the play before the fee has been paid and the licence issued.**

Licences are issued subject to the understanding that it shall be made clear in all advertising matter that the audience will witness an amateur performance; that the names of the authors of the plays shall be included on all announcements and on all programmes; and that the integrity of the authors' work will be preserved.

The Royalty Fee is subject to contract and subject to variation at the sole discretion of Samuel French Ltd.

In Theatres or Halls seating Four Hundred or more the fee will be subject to negotiation.

In Territories Overseas the fee quoted in this Acting Edition may not apply. A fee will be quoted on application to our local authorized agent, or if there is no such agent, on application to Samuel French Ltd, London.

VIDEO-RECORDING OF AMATEUR PRODUCTIONS

Please note that the copyright laws governing video-recording are extremely complex and that it should not be assumed that any play may be video-recorded for *whatever purpose* without first obtaining the permission of the appropriate agents. The fact that a play is published by Samuel French Ltd does not indicate that video rights are available or that Samuel French Ltd controls such rights.

CHARACTERS

Beattie Gladwin, aged eighty
Polly Bradbury, aged seventy-three
Michelle Druitt, aged twenty-seven
Brian Martin, aged thirty-two

The action of the play takes place in a front room

Time—the present

Production Note

In order to achieve the maximum dramatic effect from Beattie's entrance and exit during Scene 2, the swivel chair should be placed close to the fireplace, so that Beattie can enter and exit either through the fireplace or around the flats supporting it.

THE HOUSEWARMING

Scene 1

The front room of 10 Albany Road

There is a free-standing window and a fireplace. Entrances DL and R lead to the front hall and the kitchen respectively. The only furniture is a tea chest serving as a seat or a table, and a large, dilapidated swivel easy chair. There are curtains at the window, and a framed print hangs above the fireplace

When the Curtain rises, the Lights come up on Beattie, sitting in the chair, looking around the empty room

Polly enters from the kitchen, R. She is drying her hands on a towel. She looks at Beattie for a moment or two

Polly Don't sit there feeling sorry for yourself.
Beattie I will, if I want to.
Polly I'm nearly finished in the kitchen. Are you ready to go?
Beattie What are we doing with that picture?
Polly I thought we'd leave it for the new people.
Beattie Why?
Polly Well... A sort of welcoming present.
Beattie You didn't ask.
Polly It was on the list I gave you. You didn't say you wanted it.
Beattie I don't want it.

Polly You can't keep everything. There isn't room.

Beattie I might not want to give them a present.

Polly (*going to take down the picture*) All right, we'll take it with us.

Beattie Leave it.

Polly I'll put it in the dustbin.

Beattie No! They can do that if they don't want it.

Polly (*turning away*) Oh dear.

Beattie It was a wedding present from his workmates. Frame's worth more than the picture.

Polly They often are. I'll just finish tidying up. (*She moves* DR)

Beattie It's not right, Polly.

Polly (*turning*) I know dear. Better if you hadn't come.

Beattie It's my house. I wanted to say goodbye. Never seen it like this though—without furniture.

Polly You must have.

Beattie No. Frank furnished it before we moved in. He did it all. Our dream home he called it.

Polly And it was.

Beattie What a short memory you have.

Polly It's how it always seemed to me.

Beattie I loved this house. It should've been happy ever after.

Polly There were many happy times here, for all of us. I remember them even if you don't.

Beattie These people you've sold it to—what are they like?

Polly They're nice—pleasant people.

Beattie All been done behind my back. Why have they got different names?

Polly Because they're not married, I suppose.

Beattie Are they getting married?

Polly I don't know. It's none of our business. You'd like them. Really you would.

Beattie I should never have agreed to sell. They'll probably tear the place to bits.

Scene 1

Polly Not necessarily.

Beattie Young people are all the same. Can't wait to rip up the past.

Polly They'll want to modernize the house, yes. It's only natural.

Beattie (*angrily*) It doesn't need modernising. It suited me for sixty years.

Polly Oh Beattie, play a different tune.

Beattie Listen.

Polly Come on, let's——

Beattie (*interrupting*) Shush—listen!

Pause

Polly I can't hear anything.

Beattie A voice—a girl's voice, calling.

Polly It's the children playing in the street.

Beattie She's in the back garden. I can hear her.

Polly There's no-one in the garden. You're imagining things.

Beattie One day—one day I know she'll come back.

Polly Oh Beattie, stop torturing yourself.

Beattie struggles to find her handkerchief. Polly gives her hers. Beattie wipes her eyes

Come on, let's get you back for your tea.

Beattie Sardines on toast yesterday.

Polly That was nice.

Beattie No, it wasn't. I haven't had a decent meal since I went to live in that place.

Polly That's not true. Some of the meals are very good.

Beattie They ought to be—the price I pay.

Polly You won't have to worry about money any more—not now the house is sold.

Beattie If you were so happy here, Polly, why wouldn't you stay and look after me?

Polly You never let go, do you! I've told you, Beattie, I'm too old to nurse people—even my own sister.
Beattie (*trying to stand*) Help me up.

Polly crosses to help her to her feet

Beattie Stupid chair! Far too low.
Polly Come on—nearly there.

With Polly supporting her, Beattie stands upright

Beattie (*breathing heavily*) Frank's retirement present—a lousy swivel chair. I've always hated it.
Polly I couldn't find anyone to take it.
Beattie We're giving them that as well, I suppose. When do they move in?
Polly They're collecting the keys tomorrow.
Beattie Couldn't they have waited until I'm dead?
Polly Don't talk like that.
Beattie I wanted to die here.
Polly You do say some silly things.
Beattie We promised each other we'd both die here, Frank and me.
Polly You can't make promises like that.
Beattie He got his way, didn't he? (*She sniffs*) I can smell gas.
Polly (*sniffing*) A faint smell. Nothing.
Beattie Better turn it off.
Polly Not necessary, but if it makes you happy… (*She moves* DR, *towards the kitchen door*)
Beattie Can I see the garden before I go?
Polly (*turning*) I've just locked the back door.
Beattie I'll look through the kitchen window. That's all I want to do.

Polly (*moving back to her*) Oh what a pest you are. Come on, then.

They start to move DR

Beattie I keep thinking. Suppose—suppose she comes back and there's no-one here.
Polly She can't come back. Why won't you understand?
Beattie I never wanted to sell this house.
Polly (*impatiently*) If you can't look after yourself, Beattie, you can't live here.
Beattie But I could die here. That's all I want.

They exit R, *as the Lights fade to Black-out*

SCENE 2

Next day. Late afternoon sun shines through the windows

Michelle Druitt runs in from L. *She is happy. She looks around and then moves to the window to look out*

Brian Martin enters L, *carrying a cardboard box. His viewing of the room is a little more critical. He puts the box on the floor*

Michelle turns. She runs to Brian and puts her arms around his neck

Michelle Well, this is it.
Brian Yes. For better or worse.
Michelle It's lovely and it's ours.
Brian I know. We've got a mortgage to prove it.

Michelle And there's so much we can do to it. Isn't it exciting?
Brian (*moving from her*) It looks different without the furniture.
Michelle I know you, Brian. You'll be looking for the woodworm and the dry rot.
Brian Not to mention the rising damp.
Michelle The survey said it was sound in wind and limb.
Brian With broken guttering and rotting window frames.
Michelle Minor details.
Brian Says she.
Michelle Daddy knows someone who'll deal with the windows.
Brian I'll cope, thank you. No need to call the cavalry.
Michelle Eh! Why so touchy?
Brian I dunno. It all seems so second hand.
Michelle Better than that grotty flat.
Brian I'll grant you that. Oh, it'll be all right once we get started.
Michelle (*swinging the chair around*) I wonder why they left this? (*She sits in the chair*)
Brian Looks pretty clapped-out to me.
Michelle We could tart it up a bit.
Brian No, thanks. We'll tip it.
Michelle Be useful while we're decorating. When we have our elevenses. What's in the box?
Brian (*lifting the tea chest lid*) Empty, more or less.
Michelle You can tip that.
Brian Not likely. Tea chests are valuable. (*He takes a newspaper from the tea chest*) Even left us some reading matter. (*He replaces the lid and puts the newspaper on top*)
Michelle (*standing*) All right, lord and master, where do we start?
Brian (*moving to her*) We could try out the bedroom.
Michelle Oh yes?
Brian Do you think they've left a bed behind as well?
Michelle (*slipping away from him*) Let's hope not. Otherwise there'll be no work done.

Scene 2

Brian Too much work and no play makes Michelle a dull girl.
Michelle At the moment Michelle is thinking about the kitchen. Like, what colour shall we paint it?
Brian Bright primrose?
Michelle Ugh! With those tiles?
Brian Ah yes.
Michelle A warm pink, all over—ceiling as well.
Brian Whatever...
Michelle No, Bri, we have to agree.
Brian Pink's fine, if it makes you happy.
Michelle Oh yes, I'm happy. Our house. I can't believe it.
Brian I love you. (*He takes her hand*) Let's go and look at the bedroom.
Michelle (*breaking away; laughing*) You...
Brian Come on.
Michelle In a minute. Decisions first.
Brian More decisions?
Michelle Like deciding how long we're going to live here.
Brian You can't decide things like that.
Michelle Yes we can. Do you think the children will like it here?
Brian Hold on, girl. One step at a time. We haven't painted the kitchen yet.
Michelle No, no, come on. Think ahead.
Brian Well—as I see it—the children...
Michelle Go on.
Brian They'll be born here; perhaps start school from here, but... I don't know—I can't see this place suiting us forever.
Michelle I think I could live here till I die. That's how I feel. (*She moves to him*)
Brian (*hugging her*) What are you talking about? Dying!

About to kiss, they are startled by a long, loud ring of the doorbell

At least the doorbell works.

Michelle I wonder who that is. (*She runs to the window*)
Brian Ten to one it's your family. Or Jehovah's Witnesses. I'll settle for Jehovah.
Michelle It's Miss Bradbury.
Brian What does she want?
Michelle Soon find out. (*She goes* L) And be polite. She's quite harmless.

Michelle exits L

Brian moves to the fireplace and looks at the picture above it. The room gets slowly darker during the following scene

Michelle (*off*) Hallo, Miss Bradbury. Do come in.
Polly (*off*) I hope I haven't come at an inconvenient time.
Michelle (*off*) No, of course not. Go in. Brian's here as well.

Polly enters

Polly (*speaking as she enters*) Only I saw the car outside and there are one or two things I need to explain. Hallo, Mr Martin.
Brian Hallo again. How are you?
Polly You've noticed the picture.
Brian Er—yes. Did you want it?
Polly No, no. My sister thought... Well, we both thought that we'd like to make you a little... Well, it's not a lot, I know, but a sort of welcoming present.
Brian Oh right, I see—yes.
Michelle (*crossing to the fireplace*) It's very kind of you. We shall treasure it. Thank you.
Brian Yes—thanks.
Polly It's been hanging there since my sister got married. It was a wedding present but she thought... We both thought—that it belonged here and you... Well, you might...

Scene 2

Awkward pause

Michelle What was it you wanted to talk to us about, Miss Bradbury?
Polly Oh yes... What I really came for—was to apologize.
Michelle Apologize? What for?
Polly The mess in the kitchen for a start. We had a little accident with the gas.
Brian What sort of accident?
Polly The wall needs scraping or scrubbing. We didn't have the time. I'm really very sorry.
Brian I'll just take a look.

Brian exits R

Michelle Don't worry, Miss Bradbury. We'll see to it.
Polly I suppose you'll be doing a lot of painting and things.
Michelle Oh yes, we've lots to do... Lots of plans.
Polly I hope you don't mind me saying this, but you're very pretty.
Michelle Pardon?
Polly You remind me of someone—dead now, alas.

Brian returns

Brian See what you mean. Bit of a mess. Did you have a fire or what?
Polly I'll help you clean it up—gladly.
Michelle No, that won't be necessary.
Polly I feel so awful about it.
Brian Don't worry yourself. It's one of those things. We have to wash it all down before we can decorate anyway.
Polly You're very understanding, Mr Martin. Thank you. And I'm very sorry about the blood.

Michelle Blood!
Brian Pardon?
Michelle What blood? Where?
Polly Well, bloodstain, I mean. It's dry now, but we scrubbed and scrubbed. I don't know why, but we couldn't seem to move it. (*She points*) There—in front of the fireplace.
Michelle Oh! (*She steps back in alarm*)

Pause. Brian and Michelle look where Polly pointed

Brian Here?
Polly Yes. It's where Frank—that's Mrs Gladwin's husband—he collapsed. I was here at the time, but there was nothing anyone could do.
Michelle (*looking at the spot*) I can't see any...

Michelle stops as she notices Brian with his finger to his lips

Brian Look, Miss Bradbury, a piece of carpet will soon cover that. So don't worry. The roof's on and the windows are intact. Everything else we'll cope with.
Polly Yes, of course you will. By the way, we left the curtains. They help to make the place look occupied, even when it's empty, don't you think?
Brian Yes—thank you very much. Anything else?
Polly I'll go now. I've been a nuisance for long enough. You know where my flat is—just round the corner—if you want me.
Brian (*ushering her to the exit* L) I'm sure we won't need to bother you.
Michelle Oh, Miss Bradbury, when you see Mrs Gladwin, tell her how pleased we are with the picture.
Polly (*turning*) I'm sorry?
Michelle Your sister... When you see her...
Polly My sister? Oh yes, yes, I'll tell her. It's been nice meeting

Scene 2

you, Miss Druitt. I'll see you again, no doubt. Goodbye, Mr Martin.

Michelle Goodbye. And thank you.

Polly and Brian exit L

(*Laughing*) Thank you? What for, for goodness sake? (*She stands staring at the spot in front of the fireplace*)

She runs R and exits into the kitchen

Brian (*off*) Goodbye.

Brian returns

Let's hope she doesn't make a habit of visiting. (*He looks around*) 'Chelle?

Michelle appears DR

Michelle God, Brian, what a mess.
Brian Yes, a right pig's breakfast.
Michelle We're lucky they didn't burn the house down.
Brian Very cagey about how it happened, wasn't she?
Michelle (*moving to him*) That's rubbed the shine off things. It'll take ages to get it cleaned.
Brian (*putting his arms around her*) Eh… What's become of the happy home owner?
Michelle Just wondering what else we'll find.
Brian (*flippantly*) A few bloodstains perhaps. Nothing to worry about.
Michelle That's another thing. There isn't any blood. Why did you…?
Brian No good arguing with her, was it?

Michelle But what was it all about?

Brian Search me.

Michelle It's almost as if she was trying to frighten us.

Brian Take more than a confused old crone like Miss Bradbury to do that.

Michelle I'm just beginning to realize. This house—it's older than we are and it knows more than we do.

Brian Yes, well... What it knows it can keep to itself. I'm thirsty. So how about a cuppa?

Michelle Did you pack the kettle?

Brian (*pointing*) In the box.

Michelle (*moving from him*) Right, then tea you shall have. (*She picks up the box and moves* R, *towards the kitchen*)

Brian I'll get the rest of the things from the car.

Michelle (*turning*) Bri! Don't let's stay late tonight.

Brian No... we'll just do a quick survey, decide on a plan of action and then get back to the flat. OK?

Michelle Yes, please.

Brian Besides, I fancy you.

Michelle (*laughing*) Tell me something new.

Michelle exits R

Brian stands for a moment, looking at the floor, then he picks up the newspaper and starts to read it

Michelle re-enters, holding a small table-cloth

Michelle Always got your nose stuck in a newspaper.

Brian What? Oh yeah, can't resist 'em.

He puts the newspaper down on the chair and exits L. *Michelle lays the table-cloth over the tea chest and then exits* R *to the*

Scene 2

kitchen. Brian re-enters, carrying a box. He deposits it on the floor. Seeing the table-cloth, he smiles. He exits again. Michelle returns with two beakers and two plates, which she sets on the box. She picks up the newspaper and glances at it. Something attracts her attention and she starts to read. Brian returns with a second box. He puts it down

Michelle Eh, Bri, did you read this——
Brian (*interrupting*) She hasn't gone away, you know.
Michelle Who?
Brian Miss—what's her name—Bradbury. Standing on the other side of the road, staring at the house.
Michelle (*dropping the newspaper*) Close the curtains.
Brian Pardon?
Michelle Close the curtains. I don't want people looking in at us.
Brian OK, love, keep calm. (*He moves to the window and draws the curtains*)

The room is instantly darkened

Michelle Oh God, no! Where's the light switch?
Brian Whoo-oo-ooo. I'm coming to get you.
Michelle No, no, Brian, don't. Please.
Brian (*barking his shin on the tea chest*) Ouch!
Michelle Serves you right.
Brian You can't escape, my little maiden. I have you in my clutches.
Michelle Brian, stop it. Do you hear? I'm frightened.

The Lights come on. Brian is standing by the light switch, near the entrance L

I'm sorry. What the hell is the matter with me?

Brian It's all right. (*He goes to her*) That silly old bat's put you a bit on edge, that's all. (*He puts his arm around her*)
Michelle Kiss me.

He kisses her. The swivel chair turns to reveal Beattie, sitting watching them

Michelle breaks from Brian's embrace

Now you can have your cup of tea.
Beattie Would you have a spare cup by any chance?

Brian and Michelle turn. Michelle screams and clings to Brian

Brian What the... Who the hell are you?
Beattie I looked through the window. It seemed such a warm house.
Brian Yes, maybe, but if you wouldn't mind...
Michelle It's not your house.
Brian (*moving to Beattie*) Come on, out!
Beattie My name's Beattie. I don't have a house anymore.
Brian I'm sorry, but it still doesn't give you the right to come in here.
Beattie You must be the new owners.
Michelle That's right.
Beattie This isn't just a house. It's a home. I can tell. There's love here. Don't you two ever fall out of love.
Michelle We'll try not to.
Beattie Promise yourselves. You see, when love goes... (*She stops, staring straight ahead*)
Michelle Are you all right?
Beattie (*smiling*) Just worn out, my dear. That's all.
Brian You're not welcome here. And if you don't leave at once by the way you came in, I shall throw you out.

Scene 2 15

Michelle Brian! At least let's give her a cup of tea.

Beattie You're very kind.

Brian Oh sure—open house! I'll pop out into the street and bring a few more beggars in.

Michelle Don't talk like that. It's pathetic.

Brian (*shamed*) Well... Just make sure she stays in your half of the house.

Michelle (*laughing*) Right! Will you draw the line or shall I?

Beattie There was a lot of laughter in this house years ago.

Brian How would you know?

Beattie If you listen carefully, you can hear it still.

Brian Oh, really!

Beattie Don't think, Mr Martin, just because the house has been empty, that all the memories have gone as well.

Brian Pardon?

Beattie smiles

How come you know my name?

Beattie People talk. "Who's buying the house?" they ask. And someone always knows.

Michelle So you knew Mrs Gladwin—the lady who used to live here?

Beattie Of course I did.

Michelle And Mr Gladwin?

Beattie Yes, I knew him. Curly hair and twinkly eyes. Surprising how a smile hides the truth sometimes.

Michelle What do you mean?

Beattie Impossible to forget—or forgive. God knows I tried. But don't you worry yourselves. This house will make you both very happy.

Michelle Did they have any children?

Brian I don't want my happiness decided by other people.

Michelle What's the matter with you? Calm down.

Beattie Children, yes. Lots of them running about, shouting to one another. And a special little girl, Stella. Such a pretty little thing, always laughing. I can hear her laughing now.
Michelle Tell me about her.
Beattie It was an accident.
Michelle What was?
Beattie An accident. Could have happened to anyone.
Brian How long's this going on—all this history?
Michelle I happen to be interested. OK?
Beattie You can't ignore the past, Mr Martin. It's the only thing in life you can be sure of.
Brian She'll be saying it's haunted next.

Beattie laughs

> I'm going to make the tea. The sooner she has her cuppa and goes on her way, the better.

Brian exits R

Michelle I'm sorry. Brian isn't normally like that.
Beattie Men, my dear, like to think they create the world from nothing every day. But we know better, don't we? You can't clean the memories out of your mind, and you can't clean the memories out of this house.
Michelle Tell me what happened to the little girl.
Beattie The house knows. Listen to it. It'll tell you.

The Lights go out. Michelle screams. Beattie laughs

Brian (*off*) Damn!
Michelle (*calling*) Brian, what's happened?

Brian enters

Scene 2   17

Brian (*entering*) Switched the kettle on and bang…! Fuse, I suppose. Where's that second box? There are a couple of torches in it.
Michelle Over here. Are you all right, Beattie?
Beattie All right, my dear? Of course. Don't worry about me.
Brian (*rummaging through the box*) Don't worry about her. I'll have the surveyor's guts. They're supposed to check things like electrics. Right! Here we are. And one for you.

They switch on their torches

Michelle So much for our cup of tea. I'm sorry, Beattie.

Michelle shines her torch on the chair, but it's empty

Beattie!

Brian and Michelle swing their torches around the room

Brian That's one problem solved.
Michelle But where has she gone? She didn't go past me.

Brian shines his torch on the chair, and then up at the wall above the fireplace. The picture is not there

Brian Look. She's taken that damned picture.
Michelle Of all the nerve!
Brian Good riddance. We didn't want it anyway.
Michelle But where did she go?
Brian The kitchen.

Brian exits R

Michelle swings her torch around the room

Michelle (*calling softly*) Beattie. Beattie.

Brian returns

Brian Thought she might be mending the fuse for us. But no such luck.
Michelle Do you know what I think?
Brian Go on, Sherlock, sock it to me.
Michelle Don't ask me to explain, but I think that Beattie is Mrs Gladwin... The lady we bought the house from.

Slight pause

Brian Possible, I suppose. In which case, what's she doing here?
Michelle Perhaps she finds it hard to let go. I could understand that.
Brian More likely she popped in to give us the once-over. See whether we're fit to live in her house.
Michelle (*laughing*) What a pity you behaved so badly.
Brian I did no such thing.
Michelle Doesn't matter. Let's leave it till the morning. It'll look different in broad daylight.
Brian I'll mend the fuse first.
Michelle No, let's go home.
Brian There's some fuse wire in the tool box in the car.
Michelle Please, Bri.
Brian It'll still need mending in the morning. It won't take long.
Michelle Well—hurry.
Brian Just sit in the chair and don't move.

Brian exits L

Michelle moves about in the dark. She stops

Scene 2

Michelle Beattie, Beattie, are you there? (*She pauses*) God, what's the matter with me? Stupid.

Brian re-enters

Brian?
Brian Key, please.
Michelle Pardon?
Brian Key to the front door. You were the last one to come in.
Michelle I left it in the lock.
Brian It's not there now.
Michelle It must be.
Brian And we're locked in.
Michelle Oh no. The floor. It'll have fallen on the——
Brian (*interrupting*) No. I looked.
Michelle Anyway, where's your key?
Brian In my anorak.
Brian
Michelle } (*together*) In the car!
Brian Fancy spending the night here?
Michelle No, I don't. If we can't get out of the door, we'll go through the window. (*She draws back the curtains*)

Someone is standing outside, a silhouette, backlit

She screams

Brian! (*She pulls the curtains shut*)
Brian (*moving to her*) Don't do that, girl.
Michelle (*clinging to him*) There is someone outside.
Brian There's a whole world outside if we get a chance to join 'em.
Michelle She was there. Someone...
Brian She?
Michelle Beattie, or Miss Bradbury.

Brian Bloody peeping Toms. (*He flings back the curtains*)

Light from a street lamp shines through the window

No-one there now.
Michelle I saw someone.
Brian Yes, well, you must have frightened them away. Let's escape. (*He tries to open the window*)
Michelle Hurry up.
Brian I'm trying to. It's stuck. Paint like glue all round the frame. (*He hits the frame with his fist*) It won't budge.
Michelle Break the glass. Here, use my shoe.
Brian Eh, steady on. That's not necessary. There is such a thing as a back door, you know.
Michelle Come on then, let's go. (*She hurries across the stage*)

The Lights come back on. The picture is back in place

Oh?

Brian Great Scott! Let there be light.
Michelle Thank God! I was beginning to think... (*She goes to him*) I'm sorry I panicked. I love you, Bri.
Brian Yeah—me you. (*He glances around the room*)
Michelle (*laughing*) Isn't it bright. (*She looks at him*) What's the matter?
Brian One simple question. Why did the lights come back on?
Michelle Someone put money in the meter.
Brian Very funny.
Michelle It must have been a power cut.
Brian Just at the moment I switched the kettle on? Bit of a coincidence.
Michelle It's not impossible.
Brian And how do you account for that? (*He points at the picture*)
Michelle What? What am I supposed to be looking at?

Scene 2

Brian The picture. It's back.

Michelle So it is.

Brian Any ideas?

Michelle (*breaking from him*) I don't know, do I? Perhaps it wasn't missing at all. Perhaps we shone our torches in the wrong place.

Brian It was missing all right. You know it was. (*He moves to the fireplace and examines the picture frame*)

Michelle There must be a logical explanation.

Brian Yes, but I'm damned if I know what it is. (*He picks up the newspaper and sits in the chair*)

Michelle I wonder if the front door key's come back as well.

Michelle exits L

Brian glances at the newspaper. Something attracts his attention and he begins to read

Brian (*calling; excitedly*) 'Chelle. 'Chelle, look at this. (*He gets up and moves towards the hall doorway L*)

Polly enters R. She carries a bucket

Brian turns and sees her

Brian (*moving towards her*) Miss Bradbury, what are you doing here?

Polly Out of my way. You've done enough damage already. (*She crosses to the fireplace*)

Brian Look, I need some explanations.

Polly ignores him. She kneels down in front of the fireplace, takes a brush from the bucket and starts to scrub the floor, hard. Brian throws the newspaper on the chair

Miss Bradbury, can you hear me? Stop scrubbing now. There's nothing there.

Polly (*not looking at him*) You would say that, wouldn't you.

Beattie enters L

We can hardly expect you to face up to what you've done.

Brian All right, Miss Bradbury, what have I done?

Polly (*seeing Beattie*) You're back! What did they say?

Beattie They may want to see us again.

Polly Me as well?

Beattie Yes.

Polly Then we must talk about it. Make sure we tell the same story. Just children playing games.

Beattie What about him?

Polly Yes—what about him? Tell them he was out shopping. (*To Brian*) Shopping, all right?

Beattie I think we should just tell the truth.

Polly If you do, they'll take him away. (*She pauses*) Is that what you want? You'll lose everything.

Beattie (*removing her coat*) I don't want any more misery. Haven't I suffered enough?

Beattie exits, carrying her coat

Brian Miss Bradbury, why are you here? This is our house now. Why can't you leave us alone?

Polly gets to her feet

If this is some sort of trick, we'll go to the police.

Polly We're in a mess, Frank—a terrible mess. I don't know what we're going to do. But whatever it is, don't forget—I love you. (*She kisses him on the cheek*)

Scene 2

Beattie re-enters

Beattie You two never miss a chance, do you?

Polly Would you prefer me to hate him?

Beattie (*looking at the floor in front of the fireplace*) I can still see the marks.

Polly I've scrubbed all I'm going to. No-one'll see anything.

Beattie I shall see it for the rest of my life. (*She collapses into the chair*) Oh God, how do we keep going? What sort of future is there?

Polly Pull yourself together, Beattie. We'll get over it.

Beattie It's all right for you. She wasn't your daughter.

Polly But I loved her as if she was.

Beattie I don't think any of us loved her in the right way. Not enough to save her.

Polly That's silly talk. What's done is done. We have to come to terms with it.

Polly exits L

Brian moves to Beattie

Brian Beattie. Beattie, we must talk. (*He kneels beside the chair*)

Beattie We could have been so happy here, you and me. Without her, of course—dear sister. Did she corrupt you Frank? Or were you already on the path to hell? We shall never know, shall we? You were in here with Polly and Stella. I was at a neighbour's house. I heard Stella screaming as she ran into the street. Why, Frank? What had you done to her? I ran up the road—arms, legs useless against the wind. But a car, a big, black car came fast round the corner. (*Shouting*) Stella! (*She pauses*) They carried her in from the street and laid her down there. If only she would speak to me. But nothing. Her little face twisted... Blood drying on her clothes. You've taken my Stella from me and I loathe and detest you. (*She pulls his hair, jerking back his head*) For that, one day, God help me, I'll kill you both. (*She releases her grip, gets up and moves to the window*) Without my little girl this house is a tomb. I'm waiting—every day I'm waiting for her to come back. I shan't leave here until she does. (*She moves towards the hall doorway* L)

Brian Beattie, listen to me. It's not our fault. Leave us alone.

Beattie exits as Brian moves towards her

Brian stands staring after her

Michelle enters from the hallway

Michelle It was there all the time. (*She pauses*) Brian?
Brian What?
Michelle The key—it was there. I've unlocked the door. We can escape.
Brian It's our house, 'Chelle. We shouldn't need to escape.
Michelle What's the matter?
Brian They were here, both of them.
Michelle Here?
Brian Beattie and that Miss Bradbury.
Michelle I thought it was me who was seeing things.
Brian They were here, I tell you. They talked to me.
Michelle So where are they now?
Brian They went out.

Michelle goes towards the kitchen door

Not that way. Through the hall.
Michelle Oh, you mean those two old biddies I just bumped into?
Brian 'Chelle!

Scene 2

Michelle Brian, you're imagining things.

Brian I wish I was.

Michelle Well, I didn't see them—or hear them. And I was only in the hall for a few seconds.

Brian I remember calling you but...

Michelle All right, what did they say this time? More anecdotes?

Brian It doesn't matter.

Michelle Look, love, this is our house now. We're in charge. We call the tune.

Brian I wonder whether it'll ever be ours—properly ours.

Michelle When they come back, I shall tell them.

Brian I was... I was wondering...

Michelle Go on.

Brian Whether this place is so important after all—to us, I mean.

Michelle We paid out a lot of money and our names are on the deeds. Isn't that important enough?

Brian What I mean is... The estate agent said he always has plenty of houses like this on his books——

Michelle (*interrupting*) Sell you mean? Even before we move in? Over my dead body.

Brian It's no good if we're not happy here.

Michelle But I am happy. At least I was until all this nonsense started.

Brian What did she say? Beattie I mean. The house was always full of children.

Michelle Yes, she said that. They came to play with Stella. One day they'll come to play with our children.

Brian No! (*He pauses*) No, they mustn't.

Michelle Eh, love? Calm down.

Brian (*mumbling*) I'm sorry.

Michelle You're frightened, aren't you?

Brian Yes. Aren't you?

Michelle Brian, things have happened since we walked into this house. Beattie in that chair—the face at the window—the face you didn't see, remember—the power cut. I jumped, I screamed. I was startled, but not scared because I don't see anything sinister. There is an explanation. Unless you know something I don't.

Brian moves to the tea chest and picks up the newspaper

Brian Look, there's something in this newspaper you should see.
Michelle About the fire? I've seen it.
Brian Fire? What fire?
Michelle In our kitchen.
Brian I didn't see anything about a fire.
Michelle So what are you talking about?
Brian I'll show you. (*He searches the front page of the newspaper*) It's a report—about Frank Gladwin's trial.
Michelle Beattie's Frank?
Brian Of this address. The police called him the Pied Piper. (*He turns to an inside page; puzzled*)
Michelle Why?
Brian Isn't it obvious?
Michelle Because the children followed him?
Brian Right. But his own daughter ran away from him and was killed in the road outside. (*He searches the pages*) Where the hell is it?
Michelle Why did she run away?
Brian They never found out why. He was acquitted. Because he lied. They all lied. I heard them planning it. (*He gives up his search*) This is the wrong newspaper.
Michelle (*taking the newspaper from him*) Let me find my story.
Brian There must be another one. (*He begins to look around the room*)
Michelle You're right. It is the wrong paper. The one I read was yesterday's.

Scene 2

Brian Couldn't have been. Frank's trial was ten years ago.
Michelle But this one, Brian, it's dated—nineteen-thirty-five.
Brian Nineteen—what? (*He moves to her*)
Michelle Look at the picture.
Brian A wedding?
Michelle (*reading*) "At All Saint's Church on Saturday last, Beatrice Bradbury to Frank Gladwin." But the paper I read was about the fire in our kitchen and two women being taken to hospital with serious burns.

A slight pause

Brian That's it then, isn't it. If they're in hospital, they can't be here. What we've been seeing can only be ghosts.
Michelle Or a couple of old tricksters trying to frighten us out of the place.
Brian Oh, my love, I wish it was that simple. When you move into a house, it should be clean—no memories, no history, right? But this one isn't, is it? It's full of lies and guilt. If we stay, we'll be saddled with it.

Michelle shakes her head

Do you understand?
Michelle (*quietly*) Rubbish, Brian. I'm not being saddled with anything.

Beattie enters from the hall. Brian sees her, but Michelle has her back to her

Come on, let's go. Tomorrow morning we'll search out Beattie and Miss Bradbury and we'll nail them to the ground. (*She turns to go, and, seeing Beattie, she jumps*)
Beattie There you are, my little Stella. I knew you'd come back.

Michelle (*moving to her*) Beattie, what's your game?
Beattie Games? Oh yes, you ask him about games. (*She pushes past Michelle*) Ask Frank.
Michelle Brian, what's she talking about?
Brian (*trying to take her hand*) Come on, 'Chelle, let's go.
Michelle Not until I get some explanations.
Brian Don't get involved.
Beattie (*turning suddenly and seizing Michelle by the wrist*) Give Mummy a big kiss. Come on, my dear. I've waited so long.
Michelle Let go of me. Stop it. You're hurting me.

Polly enters DR *at the end of Beattie's speech*

Beattie Everything I did, my little Stella, was to repay you. Oh, what rows we had, him and me. One of many, in here on Sunday afternoon. I scream out my hate for everyone to hear. I wish I could kill you! (*She pauses slightly*) And then, suddenly, the blood trickles from his mouth... And he falls—there! It's not my fault, they say. But I know, because I want to kill him, I have killed him. And I'm glad. I cried for days. And when I'm ill, Polly looks after me. Until one day the kitchen is full of gas. You can smell it in every corner. And I know—I know it's my chance. Rest in peace, my little Stella. (*She lets go of Michelle*)
Polly Come along, Stella. Come to Aunty Polly.

Michelle turns, bewildered and frightened. She looks at Polly, then Beattie, and finally at Brian

Michelle Brian, help me.

Brian does not move

Polly What games shall we play today, my little cherub?
Michelle What do they want from me?

Scene 2

Brian Run! Run away while you can.

Beattie I'm going visiting, my dear. Stay with your Aunty Polly. Don't be frightened.

Michelle I'm not frightened. This is my house.

Brian If you want this house, 'Chelle, you'll have to fight them for it.

Polly (*moving towards Michelle*) Aunty Polly and Daddy play games. Come and join me, Stella.

Beattie And when I get back, if you're a good girl, you can have some chocolate.

Michelle What do you want? Tell me.

Beattie (*moving towards her*) Come to Mummy, Stella. I swear I didn't know. I thought you were safe. Give me a kiss!

Polly Stella was naughty. Stella must be punished. It was only a game. Please forgive me.

Michelle I'm not Stella. Leave me alone.

Beattie I didn't know—I swear it.

Polly
Beattie } (*together*) Forgive me!

Polly It's only a game.

Michelle (*shouting*) No! No! No!

She tries to break away as they advance on her. She pushes against Polly and Beattie, but cannot escape. Finally she shoves Brian aside

  Michelle rushes to exit DL *and leaves*

Beattie Don't run away, Stella. Please don't go.
Brian 'Chelle! 'Chelle, be careful. Michelle!

  Brian exits after her

A door slams off stage. A screech of car brakes off stage. Silence

Polly (*at the window*) They'll be back.

Beattie (*sitting in the chair*) Or someone like them. Trespassers!

Polly She looked like Stella, didn't you think?

Beattie Not really. No-one does.

Polly Time to go.

Beattie I can smell gas. It's everywhere.

Polly (*sniffing*) I can't smell anything.

Beattie Better turn it off.

Polly Not necessary. But if it makes you happy. (*She moves* DR)

Beattie I don't want people in this house, trampling all over my memories.

Polly (*turning*) It isn't your house anymore. If you can't look after yourself, you can't live here.

Polly exits R

Beattie But I could die here. We could both die here. Then I need never leave. (*She fumbles in her pocket and takes out a box of matches. She opens it, takes out a match and strikes it. She holds the match up in front of her*)

The Lights fade to Black-out

CURTAIN

FURNITURE AND PROPERTY LIST

Scene 1

On stage: Tea chest with a lid. *In it:* newspaper
Large, dilapidated swivel easy chair
Window curtains are opened
Framed print set above the fireplace

Off stage: Towel (**Polly**)

Personal: **Polly**: handkerchief

Scene 2

Off stage: Cardboard box (**Brian**)
Table-cloth (**Michelle**)
Cardboard box. *In it:* 2 torches (**Brian**)
2 beakers & 2 plates (**Michelle**)
Bucket. *In it:* brush and water (**Polly**)

During Black-out on page 16

Strike: Framed print

Just before lights come back on page 20

Re-set: Framed print

Personal: **Beattie**: matches

LIGHTING PLOT

Scene 1

To open: General lighting

Cue 1 **Beattie** and **Polly** exit Fade to Black-out	(Page 5)

Scene 2

To open: Late afternoon sun shines through the window

Cue 1 **Michelle:** "Do come in." Slowly fade down during the following scene	(Page 8)
Cue 2 **Brian** draws the curtains Lights down	(Page 13)
Cue 3 **Michelle:** "I'm frightened." Bring up general lighting	(Page 13)
Cue 4 **Beattie:** "It'll tell you." Lights down. Street lamp effect outside window	(Page 16)
Cue 5 **Brian** and **Michelle** switch on their torches Bring up covering lights	(Page 17)
Cue 6 **Michelle:** "Come on then, let's go." Bring up general lighting	(Page 30)
Cue 7 **Beattie** holds the match up in front of her Fade to Black-out	(Page 30)

EFFECTS PLOT

Cue 1 **Brian** and **Michelle** are about to kiss (Page 7)
Long, loud doorbell

Cue 2 After **Brian** exits (Page 29)
Door slams. Car brakes screech

Printed by
The Kingfisher Press, London NW10 6UG